THE DEFINITIVE GUIDE TO CREATIVE WRITING AND MEDIA PRODUCTIONS

THE DEFINITIVE GUIDE TO CREATIVE WRITING AND MEDIA PRODUCTIONS

LEON LOWE

To order additional copies of this book, contact:
Xlibris
800-056-3182
www.Xlibrispublishing.co.uk
Orders@Xlibrispublishing.co.uk
721534

Wuning productions
Employment contracts

Department manger
Pre-production
Children's productions
Deliver morning television for the viewing purpose of a younger audience conveying the important topic of health safety hygiene with clarity as the point of the subject. Sunrise is a pre-production writing department so any body hired to write for sunrise must complete module assignment's to a level five standard when it is asked of them. Sunrise is for the purpose of morning television and the law is that no obscenities must be shown on morning television so the crew at sunrise productions must negotiate with these terms and conditions.

Department manager
Pre-production
Mid-Teen productions
Comical light hearted entertainment television programmes with the intention of delivering a calm refreshing look at television for youth culture and those in their primary and secondary. A focused initiative of compiling an innovative script is important for the department manager who will be assigned to work on a module for image productions, eccentricity and the ideology of fruity displays will also be key on the agenda for image productions.

Department manager
Pre-production
Family productions
Marital entertainment for family viewing conveying male to female compatibilities the values and attitudes towards companionship and family values in general. An assessment module will have to be completed also researching the topic of marriage in society typical stories will be on the agenda also.

Department manager
Pre-production
Magazine productions
Documented shows dispelling worldly ethics, informative programmes and how and why people become disabled also the raising of money to help with these peoples medical care, on this department shows will be documented and displayed in the form of game shows and paperwork assignments.

Department manager
Preproduction
Network productions
Classical storytelling of myths and legend sensible viewing for every target audience, the most adapted and worked on stories will come from timeless productions with staff compiling their most original work to craft a masterpiece of entertainment immense with nostalgia. Social morals and the ethics that are held in society will be the topic most looked at here.

Department manager
Pre-production
Ultra productions
High altitude entertainment mixing music with performance to cultivate compilations of compact disc digital versatile discs and digital versatile disc roms for the most full on release.

Department manager

Production

Logistics

Location research find suitable premises for the filming of productions look at the budget of the production and cost before deciding wither the place is suitable for filming.

Form signing sign location forms for production budget forms for cost and fees of the location filming permission forms fro the lease of premises health and safety forms for the hygiene and overall clarity of the product.

Risk assessment forms for the hazard and difficulty of the places function.

Company operations each department manager will be expected to read their contract and the company policies document that they will be asked to revise at work employees will also be assigned different tasks from time to time so it would be wise to brush up on knowledge. On set everyone will be contracted to work for five years on textbooks periodicals and media presentations for the positive growth of entertainment and the community in general.

Department manager

Production

Administration

Commissioning is to be applied for by the department managers towards the business manager for the leasing of products to distribution. This will be written on the assignment and help diagnose wither they are able to follow orders constructively without becoming rigid or to open to suggestion. When a project is commissioned it will then be sold on to a merchant trader who will put this product in the stores.

Payments will be made to various sources before administration totals it's numeration for the benefit of the employee.

Wages will be paid to department managers staff members and their employees by the ordered on their contract either weekly monthly or commissioned for the year department managers will be commissioned for the year at a base rate.

Secretary duty will be part of the administration that means filing accounts and reporting to either the bank manager or business owner for the company of a task.

Department manager
Production
Production management
Film crew liaise and communicate with each other on the direction of the production set up camera operations arrange that the health and safety risk assessments have been evaluated and work on the task of operating the duration of the production has got a good camera angle. Shoot film using camera equipment procuring safety measures through the duration ensuring that everything is in place and that they follow the script unless the director is uncertain of wither they need to make adjustments to the narrative.

Complete the finale diligently with the highest amount of discretion and remain inconspicuous all the time of their circumstance.

Department manager
Talent casting
Audition talent
Inductions
Diagnostics
Positioned
Facilitated

Department manger
Editor
Synchronize production
Validate continuity

Department manger
Distribution
Standards reviewed
Certification
Product approval
Sale to market

In this section you will learn multiple creative writing techniques it is important to know that each writing you publish becomes either a cult classic or a religious text

Anime and exotic art type scripts assignment brief

Certified scale} what and how are you trying to appeal to is it a younger or older audience who will be most interested in the topic you are involved in.

Assignment brief:
Preproduction - write a story (script)
Production — film a script
Post production review final product
Edit product.

Exotic art:
You are being assigned to write multiple productions on the art of exotica they must be sultry, clean, sensual, hypnotic, chaste, devout, productions. A exotic art script is supposed to be written at the highest standard. You're expected too right for children's and teen entertainment (mild innuendoes will be allowed but only if they are respectable and lead to positive romance). You will discuss in groups story ideas accomplishing a narrative and writing a series of five scripts in the following format.

This brief is designed with the intent guiding you through your production tasks that come in three parts the first being pre-production drafting scripts and preparing stories, the next production physically filming a script, and the final post production editing a script for the preparation of distribution.

Exotic art productions will deliver DVD movies for the viewing purpose of a younger teen audience conveying the important topic of health and safety hygiene with clarity as the subject point as well as love, romance, seduction, sensuality, freshness and relationships. Exotic art is a pre-production writing department so any body hired to write for exotic art must complete a level five-module assignment when it is asked of them. Exotic art is for the purpose of DVD television the law states that no obscenities or innuendoes must be shown on DVD television so the crew at exotic art must adhere to these terms and conditions.

Produce 66 scripts in one year.

Produce a script with the topic of a Marriage
Produce a script with the relationships
Produce a script with the topic of lovers
Produce a script with the topic of business relationship
Produce a script with the topic of fruit, food and passion
Produce a script with the topic care, benevolence and safety

Idea} the first thing you will have to do is formulate an idea for the first draft of your script this is called a narrative structure.

Topic- you will be given six different topics to write for teen children's television focus your writing skills on what you want the subject matter to be what are you going to convey on these scripts.

Concept- the theory coherent in exotic art production is teaching the youth about mundane responsibility and the importance of friendship and various child hood conceptions such as fairness and happiness make sure your characters have these representations.

Exotic art is for the purpose of teaching teenagers at a young age the importance of love and compatible closeness. Between a male and a female.

Details – when beginning on scripts it will be a good idea to detail any work referencing the main points this will able you to write the script with a clear idea in mind.

Exotic art} conversion

Sub generic genre- it will be a good idea to broaden your understanding of children's entertainment and use this in anyway possible applying this method will specify the ideas of your work. Express a vast knowledge of this understanding of children's entertainment through getting ideas together.

romance

Research development} once you have got an idea of what it is your writing about you will then have to research the story idea of your script and develop a draft.

Exotic art} conversion – LOVE BETWEEN TWO PEOPLE.

Genre- make sure you know the genre so a children's entertainment series is the genre typical of ice creams in the park and walks by the seaside or is the genre typical of bed time stories and dancing Muppet's (The genre of sunrise is children's entertainment) research the basis of children's entertainment and build a foundation.

Character- are the characters nice or are the characters smart what characteristics do the characters have for the story being conveyed.

Analogy- what happens for the beginning too the end does these analogies correspond too nature or do they correspond to sport what things are happening too fill the plot.

Metaphor- what styles attributed too the character and proverbial phrases can lend the script definition. How is this being communicated to give the story depth, use these visual representations to characterise the storyline.

Diegesis – bubble chart the story strands to increase the storyline e.g. three bubble charts telling the same story with three different point of views.

Narrative} a narrative is a pre-drafted script formulating story ideas that will initially be written as a script when the ideas have all been finalised.

Style- what method or technique are you using to write the script what approaches do you have is it presentable (mode)

Format – what is the systemic design is the lay out of your own style are they industry standard does the format construct the continuity of the story. In order to write a decent script you must remember to keep the text simple.

Theme – is the subject matter relevant and uses all the guidelines you've been working with, recheck the idea and make sure that everything has synchronised features and makes perfect sense.

Contextual language- what type of language is they using in this story what style do the dialogue have.

Genre- is the narrative type easy and simple to understand it is important to remember that you must keep your writing in a simple format.

Concise} a concise script is basically a script that keeps additional references too the rest of the story this style should be used to keep stories intrinsic.

Colour- what colours are the main concern of the topic is the scene using a lot of reds a red car a red boat or even a red table red for transport. The colour of sunrise is white and yellow, yellow for the sun white for the clouds and this must be conveyed as the atmosphere of the production.

Nature- what environment is it set in is the environment polluted a rubbish bin or is the environment clean a bathtub.

Scenery – the scenery could be kitchens were food is being prepared or the scene could be a innocent bedroom were friends are playing harmlessly. You could have a bathtub were you are cleaning a baby or you could set challenges in and around a house.

Outline - what have you realised about the scripts production does the outline of the script hold a fallible content or does the narrative need work. An outline is the basis of a completed script.

Text – how does the wording convey a children television programme is the wording intricate or is the wording simple and more easily defined, what is being said in the script that males it a children's television programme.

Basis – have you got a clever foundation for your script and is it ready too be written up as a first draft are the analogies working the way that they should.

Depiction – how does the depiction effect the story, does the characters being shown have a take on society, how are the people affecting the plot of the story.

Script}
Setting
Scene description
Character
Dialogue
Length pace duration

Draft} once you have finished the first draft of the script you will be expected to revise the scripts outcome and wither it is ready to be filmed. You will have to consider these things first.

Outline – summarize the overall script and narrative check for any flaws And make sure that everything is in place to be filmed ensuring the perfection of the narratives continuity.

Phrases – check for any phrases in the narrative and the story ensure that they are correct and in continuity with story's dialogue, remember phrases is what connects the dialogue too the story.

Analytical opinions – discuss with peers the drafted script and take note of any floors you may have then altercate these flaws swiftly.

Level – check that the script operates at the same level so if it is a level 3 colloquial such as idiom make sure you only put the same idioms in for e.g. slander which is a negative.

Topic – is the topic being conveyed one of the six topics being assigned to you through the company's logo e.g. (slumber party) (hygiene) (challenges) (cookery) freshness (care) use one of these three topics for your script.

Meaning – is the mending related to the content asked of you is the terminology relevant to your assigned task what significance has the draft got to the final product of the script.

Issue – what issues are arising is it simple and flawless or are there moments of intricate difficulty do you have too simplify the text.

Scenario} once you have finished the first draft of your script it will be important to reflect on the topic of the scenario. This is in relation too the narrative and denotes the different types of meaning being conveyed in the script.

Scene description – what type of things is going on in the scene describe the characters briefly describe the location describe the props and describe the environment (background)

Chapters – what part of the story relates too the narratives subject matter this is all in a chapter, chapter 1 may start with a girl inviting her friends chapter 2 they come over chapter 3 they settle in the party chapter 4 they eat milk and cookies e.t.c. This is all relevant of a chapter.

Point theory – what do you do when you write next to a script you have a point theory it will be a good idea to revise this point theory and think of topical phrases and anecdotes to write next to it. This can be in the form of a word graph that will be explained in to paragraphs.

Active endeavour – in the scenes of big movies there are activities that convey the stories context and active endeavour must be reflected upon to give the story its keen nature that keeps people interested.

Exotic art animation I am looking for screenwriters to get involved in the Launch of a multimedia enterprise and soon to be conglomerate. In the next two years we will take over Hollywood and become the most powerful media company in the world. I need screenwriters to help form my production company in Kent. It will be a digital media entertainment DVD company and we will make anime productions for the young and pure and also teen Adults.

The name of the genre is exotic art, It is basically what it said on the tin exotic and artful, locations must be beautiful and harmonious, the charterers must be bubbly and unique, the context must be loving and romanticized, the action is daydream fantasy with hints and streaks of comedy and eccentricity. It must be kept to Universal, parental guidance and young teen certification standards.

the main genre is romance of comedy and the sub genre is action fantasy. Use story themes tat relate to romance here are a few examples. physical attraction, Affinity, tar crossed love, impressiveness, marriage, unrequited love, obsession, infatuation, weakness, attentive partnership, jealousy, kiss, affair, passion, compassion, lust/temptation, escapism, work business dealings/money, attitude, seduction, sensuality, exoticism and eroticism.

there must be five all 2 hours 30 minutes in length, Most of all they must be romantic and bubbly with mild fantasy action. If you need any more info on the brief specify and I will help you. also send through a treatment for critiquing so I can see where you are, the treatment doesn't have to be more then a page long.

work on the narrative incorporating more ideas, what you have is negotiable but you can do better. Make the characters exuberant, the locations refreshing and exotic even if it is demons from evil lands, Make the story lines more romanticized and fantasized. right now there is no set deadline as the company has not yet launched, the launch is going to be this month, once the contracts have been signed stamped and legislated you will get paid as soon as you send the script through.

Assignment brief:
Preproduction - write a story (script)
Production – film a script
Post production review final product
Edit product

Ga – Mao productions:

This brief is designed with the intent guiding you through your production tasks that come in three parts the first being pre-production drafting scripts and preparing stories the next production physically filming a script, and the final post production editing a script for the preparation of distribution.

Produce 66 scripts in one year

Produce a script with the topic of health
Produce a script with the topic culture
Produce a script with the topic of creativity
Produce a script with the topic of relationships
Produce a script with the topic of feng shui
Produce a script with the topic of activities/pastimes

Idea} the first thing you will have to do is formulate an idea for the first draft of your script this is called a narrative. Before you formulate a narrative you will have to put together an information pack called a synopsis.

Topic – have a clear idea of the topic your going to portray and write it down this can be in the form of a theme, what subject are you going to concentrate on how does this topic give your script entertainment value. Write this topic down and begin on a word chart refer to this word chart whenever you get stuck on the subject matter of your script.

Concept – what is the concept of this idea how is it going to buff up your narrative, remember to advance the criteria knowingly.

Details – as you have written an idea and looked up the concept of the topic it is now time to put down the details of this topic make sure it is written in a simple paragraph and that any complexities are understandable.

Sub generic genre – once you have established a genre it is time to get to grips with a sub genre and split it into a critique web with many other ideas written on a web chart. Doing this will ensure that you have an understanding of the genre you are writing for. Ga – Mao is a genre on to itself, as it is a genre its sub genre is romance and it generic genre is action adventure.

Research development} once you have got an idea of what it is your writing about you will then have to research the story idea of your script and develop a draft.

This can be in the form of periodicals or just looking at the words you are writing about in a dictionary.

Genre — genre is the French word for type so research on the type of things you are going to write about, the topic of health holds the concept of beauty and good living so it would be advised that look at health and beauty magazines. The genre of Ga — Mao is family viewing so express a knowledge of family entertainment.

Character — what characteristics does culturally inclined people have

Analogy — how are your characters going to correspond to each other once you have begun on the narrative, does the idea make sense what do you know about analogies.

Metaphor — what metaphors are going to explain the way the story is written, how do you expect to get the visual image to work what do you understand about metaphors. How is this being communicated to give the story depth, use these visual representations to characterise the storyline.

Diegesis — bubble chart the story strands to increase the storyline e.g. three bubble charts telling the same story with three different point of views.

Narrative} a narrative is a pre-drafted script formulating story ideas that will initially be written as a script when the ideas have all been finalised.

Style — what methods are you going to use to make the narrative sensible? What mode is the most useful how is your understanding of style. Style on the narrative can be in the form of paragraphs or sentences that follow a vertical point theory point one once upon a time e.g. in a land far ago. Using points at intervals on the stories narrative can benefit the story's use greatly.

Format — format is an important tool when dealing with a narrative the format of a narrative can change your whole perspective of a narratives storyline and also how the layout is formatted. Format is short for formula knowing the type of format you are going to use is important a paragraph form can also explain format. The arrangement plan of the narrative and also the way the system of narrative is presented. Formula/form/format,

Theme – what is the theme of your story will it narrate what words are being used to define the meaning. Key words phrases and topical meanings convey the narrative best.

Contextual language – what is being said how does it make sense to the rest of the narrative why have you put that there what ideas are being conveyed, does the contextual language aid the narrative and work with the theme. Make sure that when you are writing the text is clear and price and that you understand the point you are trying to make.

Genre – what genre does the narrative have?

Concise} a concise script is basically a script that keeps additional references too the rest of the story this style should be used to keep stories intrinsic.

Colour – colours like flags have their own meaning, red is the colour of war and warnings, yellow is the colour of sunshine and happiness, so when your writing your scripts it would be important to remember different types of colours. Gold and purple is the best representation colour for Ga – Mao as these are the colours of romance and prestige.

Nature – what environment are the characters involved in how does this effect the story your writing, what type of things are they saying, how does this connect too the narrative.

Scenery – where are the characters located what type of things are they involved in how does this convey the theme.

Outline – where illustrations aid the script how does story give a worthy entertainment module, summarize what you have done so far does your idea make sense, will the narrative work does the idea comply with the brief.

Text – what have you written down will this be good enough to put into a script what have you written before are you ready to write the script with this text. When writing a script it is important to make sure that your audience will understand what is being said, mix complexity with simplicity, in order to understand the text must be simplified. Make your text simple as possible.

Basis – build a foundation that makes sense, illustrate with the characters that you are writing on how do they relate to the story, is it efficient, to be efficient as possible keep it simple.

Depiction – when writing a script you will have a picture in your mind of what it is your trying to convey this is called a depiction, make sure your depiction reads clearly and that everything that you are trying to say or do is made precise.

Script}
Setting
Scene description
Character
Dialogue
Length pace duration

Draft} once you have finished the first draft of the script you will be expected to revise the scripts outcome and wither it is ready to be filmed. You will have to consider these things first.

Outline – is the outline or the content suitable, does the text read well when you are reading will the depiction take smooth affect, what can you do to make the narrative illustrate in a clear detail, how does the narrative seem when you read it out can performers work with it, is the language used appropriate and avoid cliché these are all of the things you will need to look for on the scripts outline.

Phrases – what things are being said are they proverbs or casual gestures have they got hidden meanings what things can you expect form the character when after and as they say these things. What proverbs are being put in place to portray the character and are these portrayals suitable.

Analytical opinion – read through the script then take a look at the narrative making sere that everything on the pages reads as a narrative and also ensure the script has continuity to the rest of the narrative. Look at your work and other people's work critiquing wither or not it is intelligent or presentable enough to be filmed.

Level – check that the level your working at has workings you expect for instance is the piece a level 1 using simple words without much phrase or level 2 using simple words progressively, or level 3 using simple words with phrases or maybe you're a level 4 using complex words comfortably, or maybe a level 5 using complex words progressively with strong phrases.

Topic – when reading through a draft you will have to make sure that the narrative is the same narrative you started with and is the same narrative you end with, check that the topic you were working on has all the traits that you wrote down as your idea as this is the defining moment of the script.

Meaning - have you got the same meaning to the script that you started out with then its time to film the script?

Issue – raise issues with your colleagues and criticise various works,

Scenario} once you have finished the first draft of your script it will be important to reflect on the topic of the scenario.
This is in relation too the narrative and denotes the different types of meaning being conveyed in the script.

Scene description – has the script described the movement of the scene and also what is going on in the background and the general environment of the scene, how does the scene move the story along does it convey the narratives story does it relate to the characters and does the dialogue work with the scene, how does the scene function.

Chapters – scenes passages sentences all relate to duration so how much passages sentences and scenes does your story have one chapter is ten pages and on narrated footnote that would look like six chapters to a one hour script 60 pages, make sure you have this understanding of scripts.

Point theory – mark along the narrative and the script your point theory so my point theory is that a narrative with six chapters last for one hour and has sixty points to the minute if you do the calculation that's a duration of one minute to one point, write point one then begin your chapter with a one line description. E.g. once upon a time in a land far away lived a boy who conquered his village with a boring book. This is just an example of how the narration should look.

Active endeavour – how does the activity on the narrative work is the activity achievable to film if it isn't don't worry about this too much as long as the narration makes sense and conveys a story that moves along. An active endeavour is what it takes to make a film more thrilling, if it is understandable and clear in text then usually it is ready to be filmed if not work on the draft.

Certified scale} what and how are you trying to appeal to is it a younger or older audience who will be most interested in the topic you are involved in.

Target audience – Ga – Mao target audience is twelve and above.
    Various associations – kissing anecdotes and fighting metaphors
    Media entertainment – as long as people are calling in ratings Ga – Mao will work.
    Image narration innate –
    Style - Harmonious analogy

Word graph} writing can be difficult without the use of writing aids so making a word graph that relates to a theme or topic will be advised through the session.
    Chart – a word diagram that insinuates a topic can be down in a session on the white board.

Chart -
Features -
Equilibrium -
Analogy -
Metaphors -
Style -

Story objective} the objective of a story can be the most creative thing on the pages of a script, to ensure the story is entertaining you must keep an objective such as an adjective. Here are a few objectives you can take from

Retrieval
Conquest
Investigation
Survival
Achievement

Story theme} the story theme has similarities but is a different Diegesis make sure the theme of your story here are a few too keep in mind

Vengeance
Love
Honour
Justice
Revenge
A vengeances

Production}
You are being assigned by wuning productions to film a series of scripts, you will have to write a crew and cast list budget apply for a sum of money through administration find a suitable location relating to the scripts by logistics and film performers for the purpose of distributing wuning productions digital versatile discs to media companies.

You will have to get together filming permits and permission forms for the intention of showing them to property owners specifying the dates of when and how your going to make the production, once these have been signed you will then begin filming these productions for them to be sold onto media companies.

Location research – find suitable premises for the filming of productions look at the budget of the production and cost before deciding wither the place is suitable for filming.

Form signing – sign location forms for the budget of the production and budget forms for the cost and fee of the location filming permission forms for the lease of premises.

Health and safety — health and safety forms for the hygiene and overall clarity of the production set. Risk assessment forms for the hazard and difficulty of the locations function.

Company operations — each department managers will be expected to read their contract and the company policies document and will be asked to revise whilst at wuning they will be assigned different tasks whilst at wuning everyone will be contracted to work at wuning for five years on textbooks periodicals and media presentations for the positive growth of entertainment and the community in general.

Film permission forms}

Equipment checklists}

Cast crew

Travel will work in the form of travel ode and communication networking for supply and demand of location and area surveillance.

Travel costs will be put forward, through too administration and essentials sheet written up signed and dated.

A logistics manager (production officer) will be in charge of the filming and production of a feature and will have too operate the whole set.

As A LOGISTICS MANAGER AND PERSONEL YOU ARE EXPECTED TOOO TRAVEL WITH TECHNOLOGICAL EQUIPTMENT SO health and safety measure will have too be applied at all times.

Location - Location managers are responsible for all the practical arrangements involved with shooting programmers, photographs and productions outside the studio.

Productions are made in a wide range of locations; location managers need to research, identify and organize appropriate sites.

As well as arranging and negotiating site use, the role usually involves managing sites throughout the shooting process.

Research a location manager's role follows a sequence of activities from the pre-planning to completion stages of a production.

Typical activities include: Assessing scripts or storyboards and breaking them down into locations and a schedule.

Meeting with the director and designer to discuss projects; Collating ideas and undertaking research using resources such as the Internet, specialist location libraries, and local and regional film commissions/ agencies.

Producer} arrange set, communicate with film crew]

The second production team should have hints of creativity and the ability too post edit scripts so a shooting script will have too be arranged so the outlay of the location matches brief description.

Locations — locations will be networked and scoured across the country until the perfect place has been found too shoot film and record a script.

Director} direct scripts, adjust camera angles, use camera, and review script the second part of this brief is production and filming of script, as an assigned director you will have to ensure that any film script edits are done efficiently and that the filming continuity makes sense.

Writer} edit script on location, an on set write will have to ensure that the narrative is converted into a shooting script explaining camera angles so a close up, mid shoot, long shoot and landscape shoot a hand out will be provided.

Actors} read script, perform script, talent, performers will be instructed on what they have to do and be hired through various talent agencies.

Equipment} health and safety, risk assessment, hazard checks, equipment will have to be checked and safety verified so it would be an important process to take time assessing the risks of equipment and checking out the health and safety of various locations.

Script} continuity edits, film permits, the script is the most important asset and it would be advised that production managers assess the continuity and apply for a film permit via the council (wuning)
Location forms

Camera crew checklist} script editor director cast talent crew
Camera operation
Audio sound microphone
Set props
Location script
Lights day night dark light
Tracking camera equipments
Shooting script (narrative) filming

Screening

Screen theatre film analysis

Positions contract observations

Post-production}

Editing}

The final edit}

The final product}

Distribution}

Merchandising}
Assignment brief:
Preproduction - write a story (script)
Production – film a script
Post production review final product
Edit product

V – DISAH PRODUCTIONS:

This brief is designed with the intent of guiding you through your production tasks that come in three parts. The first being pre-production, drafting scripts and preparing stories. the next production physically filming a script and the final post production editing a script for the preparation of distribution.

Produce 66 scripts in one year

Produce a script with the topic of violence/communal society
Produce a script with the topic of sport
Produce a script with the topic of synchronicity/topical affairs
Produce a script with the topic of politics
Produce a script with the topic of anarchy/crime
Produce a script with the topic of disabilities

Idea} the first thing you will have to do is formulate an idea for the first draft of your script this is called a narrative structure.

Topic – think of what you want from this production label. focus on different areas utilising strengths and weaknesses within the industry and the community. How is V – diash most likely to work and on what subjects? how do you want to illustrate different facts of disabilities? This can be in the form of feature films, documentaries, periodicals, drama episodes and various other media mediums. Get a clear idea in mind then write them down on a professional note on a piece of paper.

Concept – what is the most important thing on the concept of disabilities? There are seven areas that can be worked on, how people live, how people are affected, what things are people likely to go through as a result of disability.

Details – when putting an idea of a topic together it would be wise to put every detail down and use it for the script. What to word this can be in the form of themes objectives and scenarios. Doing this enables a structure. Gathering a detailed idea requires craft and patience.

Sub generic genre – as v-disah is rather extensive it would be important to consider how this genre would do with an array of genres. A disability means you have difficulty coping in day to day life so the sub genre of anarchy would be appropriate to narrate an idea themed from this production label. When dealing with new forms of genre it can be daunting but understanding a conceptual style and design of new genres can be extremely innovative and pull in wide and varied astounded audiences.

Research development} once you have got an idea of what it is your writing about you will then have to research the story idea of your script and develop a draft.

Genre – research how different disabilities affect people and what methods there are of resolving disabilities. What things can make people feel more at ease with their inadequacies? The genre of V – disah is disabilities, so express knowledge of community strife and how people are affected by disabilities in general. In social circumstance what can be classed as a disability? You must use subversive metaphors to their full potential when developing research. (Imperative for style of genre)

Character – who are the people most at risk and what things are available to these people and also look into why people are affected by disability. Are they at odds with circumstance? Who is best placed to aid them? What methods and motives do these people portray?

Analogy — does your research correspond to the task at hand? What parallels are involved with script and story ideas? How would you define the script you are working on and why does it have the style of media your using? All these questions are somewhat rhetorical but must need to be answered in correspondence with programme content.

Metaphor — disabilities effect many people in society and can range from mental illness to physical impairment. Use this understanding to merit the differences between a well person and a person that is ill. Using metaphors to describe what it is you are conveying seems simple for this subject. E.g. love is blind, honour is deaf, freedom don't know how to walk. Take these phrases and proverbs into account and use as a visual symmetry of what it is you are trying to define.

Narrative} a narrative is a pre-drafted script formulating story ideas that will initially be written as a script when the ideas have all been finalised.

Style — when drafting a narrative make sure you have a clear idea of what it is your writing. The presentation accounts for a lot you must make sure the subject you are writing about has style and looks presentable for the final analysis.

Format — television shows are a media format. Chat shows, comedy sketch, film presentation, all of these need the correct layout. each of these has a different script type when production is looked at. The important thing is that you have a narrative for each of these or a specific story idea, be precise when drafting a narrative. V-Disah's format is usually documentaries, doc-soaps

Theme — you have a topic now what's the theme make sure you have a relevant theme and that it bares analogy to topic you have been instructed on. A theme is essential for the narrative to work so it would be important to think one up creatively. Once you have thought of one apply it to the narrative then begin drafting your script for production in three weeks.

Contextual language — when you have written the narrative make sure that the language used conveys the script story narrative of feature and that it makes sense. The context must have style be simple to understand have a clear and précised pitch and also must avoid cliché.

Genre — what type of media is it a documentary a feature film a drama episode, how does it appeal to this type of media what gives it genre, the narrative will work with the genre and in due time explain this once you have established the genre the rest of the production should fall into place as long as you have a clear understanding of what is being said.

Concise} a concise script is basically a script that keeps additional references too the rest of the story this style should be used to keep stories intrinsic.

Colour - all around the world colour has its meanings and different colours represent different things the colour red is the colour of fire war and passion, flags have different colours representing times in their history Germany is black yellow red, black for darkness, yellow for sunshine and red for a past of war. Metallic blue is the colour of V — disah and represents calm cool breeze with the suggestion of difficulty metallic rigid harsh, use this colour to convey different meanings.

Nature — what harmonious things in nature inspires you is it the blueberries or the crashes of the waves use these defining metaphors of nature to grasp an understanding of what it is you are trying to identify with, what environment does your screenplay characters surround, how do they react to their situation.

Scenery — what's happening all around the characters how come it is happening, what environment challenges do they face.

Outline —too make sure your script is concise check that the outline is the wording convenient, if not make sure you simplify any paragraphs that have become to complex putting them back on your level. If the characters become wayward make sure that you have a note of precision on their character such as their characters representation or ideology, this things determine wither their good or bad, make sure you check the work you are doing is efficient enough to be scripted if not refer to original idea.

Text – make sure everything that you have written makes sense analyse and rewrite any flaws, if the piece it's to complex it may indicate that you have to simplify the piece, make sure the work you are writing makes sense and conveys the topic you have been assigned to do, read through the text and ensure the style has analogy to the narrative.

Basis – what is the script centred on what does the script offer as a first draft, how does the script narrate' what topics give it niche, once you have established a good basis you should be able to write a good and efficient script.

Depiction – by now you should have a picture in your mind this can be converted to a metaphor if you're creative enough, once you have got a clear and precise picture in your head you can then write it into a script. Make sure your story pulls on interests and conveys twist has suspense and comical notions all of these things are important.

Script}
Setting
Scene description
Character
Dialogue
Narrative
Length pace duration

Draft} once you have finished the first draft of the script you will be expected to revise the scripts outcome and wither it is ready to be filmed. You will have to consider these things first.

Outline – does the narration on the script make sense? How do you summarize what is being said and what is being characterised,

Phrases – what are the characters saying, do they make clear remarks and communicate between each other, it is these things that you will have to look out for, how do they react, does this avoid the cliché has it got niche.

Analytical opinion – discuss with colleagues your ideas and your drafts putting them together and gathering a clear picture of what you want to be portrayed.

Level – this module is a level four so you will be expected to have a keen understanding of disabilities and work on a complex of words and have an articulate understanding of the meaning of words. V – disah covers a graphic mode of creativity and has a strong meaning of metaphor in its title. Equilibrium and the four stages carries acronym also so grasp an understanding of the text and features will be made easily.

Topic – find a topic that conveys the meaning of v –disah disability is the main topic at V – disah, writing a script will come easily once you read through this brief, how are the people affected by the disability what symmetry do they take why does this have analogy, when working on this assignment consult with colleagues to get a topic.

Meaning – what does V- disah mean, it means versus disability, who is most likely to be cruel to a disabled person why would they be cruel top a disabled person and what shape does the story take from this vindictive person. Analyse the meaning of V- disah as an acronym and analyse how the analogy corresponds with the genre.

Issue – what issues are being raised, for each of the scripts you will have to find eleven issues, that's 66 issues write these on to a word graph and use them. An issue can take many forms and are attributed to the topic, so why is the topic of a series raised this particular issue an issue with violence is abuse an issue with violence is martial art an issue with violence hospital, continue on a word graph until you reach 66 eleven for each topic.

Scenario} once you have finished the first draft of your script it will be important to reflect on the topic of the scenario. This is in relation too the narrative and denotes the different types of meaning being conveyed in the script.

Scene description – does the scene stand up to the theme ? Are you pleased with the way this works. ? How can you better it ?

Chapters – have you got sufficient topics and themes being portrayed in your chapters ? How can you ensure they are sufficient and entertaining enough to be shown to the masses ?

Point theory – review the bullet points of your themes and story strands then ensure they connect.

Active endeavours – what makes your character spectacular and stand out from the rest what obstacles have they overcome, why are they good and not bad, what makes them a winner and not a loser.

Certified scale}
Target audience -
Various associations -
Media entertainment -
Image narration innate -
Style -

Word graph} writing can be difficult without the use of writing aids so making a word graph that relates to a theme or topic will be advised through the session.

Chart – a word diagram that insinuates a topic can be done in a session on the white board. Charting words intrinsically and in a natural order can help to structure and organise the relevant plots and inevitably storyline.

Features – having various features in the forms of vignettes and anecdotes can benefit the (e.g.) entertainment value of your script giving it a natural and exciting feel. Additional features can relate to themes and story strands or just stand on there own as vignettes. All films, movies and shows can benefit from additional features but most importantly most have there own features which can relate to anything from a characters representation and ideology to the codes and conventions that drive the actual storyline/genre.

Equilibrium – the narratives structure is important always ensure story strands and plot-lines have symmetry and are believable. Equilibrium is the use of words broken down and developed into separate meanings which still bear a relation. Instead of the use of one word driving the narrative you are most likely to have four. You would usually use multiple equilibriums in a narrative.

Analogy- using words with analogy in the context of scriptwriting usually comes in the form of having a parallel ending to the beginning. An analogy is the correspondence of words usually to an outcome. Analogy would have the use of two words rather then four like equilibrium and in mundane circumstances only used once to tell the beginning and the end of a story.

Metaphors – written metaphors is important in the use of scripts. Sometimes metaphors are used without the recipient realising it. Representation of a character in the form of an anecdote is the most common form of metaphors in movies and is best suited to comedies although if used in fantasy's and other genre can be very affective inducing the scenario to a visual boost and bringing depth to story strand. A metaphor will usually work to give a story three times the effect it would have normally.

Style – the use of personal style is important wither its comedy slapstick, satirical, anecdotal, spontaneous, eccentric, sarcastic, repetitive or a silly game. In terms of romance the style could be obsession, star-crossed love, exoticism, physical attraction, affinity e.t.c. the use of styles are various and unique everyone has their own personal style as everyone is an individual.

Story objective} the objective of a story can be the most creative thing on the pages of a script, to ensure the story is entertaining you must keep an objective such as an adjective. Here are a few objectives you can take from

Retrieval
Conquest
Investigation
Survival
Achievement

Story theme} the story theme has similarities but is a different Diegesis make sure the theme of your story here are a few too keep in mind

Vengeance
Love
Honour
Justice
Revenge
A vengeances

Production}
You are being assigned by wuning productions to film a series of scripts, you will have to write a crew and cast list budget apply for a sum of money through administration find a suitable location relating to the scripts by logistics and film performers for the purpose of distributing wuning productions digital versatile discs to media companies.

You will have to get together filming permits and permission forms for the intention of showing them to property owners specifying the dates of when and how your going to make the production, once these have been signed you will then begin filming these productions for them to be sold onto media companies.

Location research – find suitable premises for the filming of productions look at the budget of the production and cost before deciding wither the place is suitable for filming.

Form signing – sign location forms for the budget of the production and budget forms for the cost and fee of the location filming permission forms for the lease of premises.

Health and safety – health and safety forms for the hygiene and overall clarity of the production set. Risk assessment forms for the hazard and difficulty of the locations function.

Company operations – each department managers will be expected to read their contract and the company policies document and will be asked to revise whilst at wuning they will be assigned different tasks whilst at wuning everyone will be contracted to work at wuning for five years on textbooks periodicals and media presentations for the positive growth of entertainment and the community in general.

Film permission forms}

Equipment checklists}

Cast crew

Travel will work in the form of travel ode and communication networking for supply and demand of location and area surveillance.

Travel costs will be put forward; through too administration and essentials sheet written up signed and dated.

A logistics manager (production officer) will be in charge of the filming and production of a feature and will have too operate the whole set.

As A LOGISTICS MANAGER AND PERSONEL YOU ARE EXPECTED TOOO TRAVEL WITH TECHNOLOGICAL EQUIPTMENT SO health and safety measure will have too be applied at all times.

Location - Location managers are responsible for all the practical arrangements involved with shooting programmers, photographs and productions outside the studio.

Productions are made in a wide range of locations; location managers need to research, identify and organize appropriate sites.

As well as arranging and negotiating site use, the role usually involves managing sites throughout the shooting process.

Research a location manager's role follows a sequence of activities from the pre-planning to completion stages of a production.

Typical activities include: Assessing scripts or storyboards and breaking them down into locations and a schedule.

Meeting with the director and designer to discuss projects. Collating ideas and undertaking research using resources such as the Internet, specialist location libraries, and local and regional film commissions/ agencies.

Producer} arranges set, communicate with film crew]

The second production team should have hints of creativity and the ability too post edit scripts so a shooting script will have too be arranged so the outlay of the location matches brief description.

Locations – locations will be networked and scoured across the country until the perfect place has been found too shoot film and record a script.

Director} direct scripts, adjust camera angles, use camera, and review script the second part of this brief is production and filming of script, as an assigned director you will have to ensure that any film script edits are done efficiently and that the filming continuity makes sense.

Writer} edit script on location, an on set write will have to ensure that the narrative is converted into a shooting script explaining camera angles so a close up, mid shoot, long shoot and landscape shoot a hand out will be provided.

Actors} read script, perform script, talent, performers will be instructed on what they have to do and be hired through various talent agencies.

Equipment} health and safety, risk assessment, hazard checks, equipment will have to be checked and safety verified so it would be an important process to take time assessing the risks of equipment and checking out the health and safety of various locations.

Script} continuity edits, film permits, the script is the most important asset and it would be advised that production managers assess the continuity and apply for a film permit via the council (wuning)

Location forms

Location forms

Camera crew checklist} script editor director cast talent crew
Camera operation
Audio sound microphone
Set props
Location script
Lights day night dark light
Tracking camera equipments
Shooting script (narrative) filming
Script editor director's cast/talent/crew

Screening

Screen theatre film analysis

Positions contract observations

Post production}

Editing}

The final edit}

The final product}

Distribution}

Merchandising}
Assignment brief:
Preproduction - write a story (script)
Production – film a script
Post production review final product
Edit product.

Sunrise productions:
    You are being assigned by wuning productions to right for its following, (sunrise productions). At sunrise productions you're expected too right for children's entertainment (no innuendoes will be allowed). You will discuss in groups story ideas accomplishing a narrative and writing a series of six scripts in the following format.

This brief is designed with the intent guiding you through your production tasks that come in three parts the first being pre-production drafting scripts and preparing stories, the next production physically filming a script, and the final post production editing a script for the preparation of distribution.

Sunrise productions will deliver morning television for the viewing purpose of a younger audience conveying the important topic of health and safety hygiene with clarity as the subject point. Sunrise is a pre-production writing department so any body hired to write for sunrise must complete a level five-module assignment when it is asked of them. Sunrise is for the purpose of morning television the law states that no obscenities or innuendoes must be shown on morning television so the crew at sunrise must adhere to these terms and conditions.

Produce 66 scripts in one year.

Produce a script with the topic of a slumber party
Produce a script with the topic of hygiene
Produce a script with the topic of challenges
Produce a script with the topic of cookery
Produce a script with the topic of fruit
Produce a script with the topic care

Idea} the first thing you will have to do is formulate an idea for the first draft of your script this is called a narrative structure.

Topic- you will be given six different topics to write for children's television focus your writing skills on what you want the subject matter to be what are you going to convey on these scripts.

Concept- the theory coherent in sunrise production is teaching the youth about mundane responsibility and the importance of friendship and various child hood conceptions such as fairness and happiness make sure your characters have these representations.

Details – when beginning on scripts it will be a good idea to detail any work referencing the main points this will able you to write the script with a clear idea in mind.

Sub generic genre- it will be a good idea to broaden your understanding of children's entertainment and use this in anyway possible applying this method will specify the ideas of your work. Express a vast knowledge of this understanding of children's entertainment through getting ideas together.

Research development} once you have got an idea of what it is your writing about you will then have to research the story idea of your script and develop a draft.

Genre- make sure you know the genre so a children's entertainment series is the genre typical of ice creams in the park and walks by the seaside or is the genre typical of bed time stories and dancing Muppet's (The genre of sunrise is children's entertainment) research the basis of children's entertainment and build a foundation.

Character- are the characters nice or are the characters smart what characteristics do the characters have for the story being conveyed.

Analogy- what happens for the beginning too the end does these analogies correspond too nature or do they correspond to sport what things are happening too fill the plot.

Metaphor- what styles attributed too the character and proverbial phrases can lend the script definition. How is this being communicated to give the story depth, use these visual representations to characterise the storyline.

Diegesis – bubble chart the story strands to increase the storyline e.g. three bubble charts telling the same story with three different point of views.

Narrative} a narrative is a pre-drafted script formulating story ideas that will initially be written as a script when the ideas have all been finalised.

Style- what method or technique are you using to write the script what approaches do you have is it presentable (mode)

Format – what is the systemic design is the lay out of your own style are they industry standard does the format construct the continuity of the story. In order to write a decent script you must remember to keep the text simple.

Theme – is the subject matter relevant and uses all the guidelines you've been working with, recheck the idea and make sure that everything has synchronised features and makes perfect sense.

Contextual language- what type of language is they using in this story what style do the dialogue have.

Genre- is the narrative type easy and simple to understand it is important to remember that you must keep your writing in a simple format.

Concise} a concise script is basically a script that keeps additional references too the rest of the story this style should be used to keep stories intrinsic.

Colour- what colours are the main concern of the topic is the scene using a lot of reds a red car a red boat or even a red table red for transport. The colour of sunrise is white and yellow, yellow for the sun white for the clouds and this must be conveyed as the atmosphere of the production.

Nature- what environment is it set in is the environment polluted a rubbish bin or is the environment clean a bathtub.

Scenery – the scenery could be kitchens were food is being prepared or the scene could be a innocent bedroom were friends are playing harmlessly. You could have a bathtub were you are cleaning a baby or you could set challenges in and around a house.

Outline - what have you realised about the scripts production does the outline of the script hold a fallible content or does the narrative need work. An outline is the basis of a completed script.

Text – how does the wording convey a children television programme is the wording intricate or is the wording simple and more easily defined, what is being said in the script that males it a children's television programme.

Basis – have you got a clever foundation for your script and is it ready too be written up as a first draft are the analogies working the way that they should.

Depiction – how does the depiction effect the story, does the characters being shown have a take on society, how are the people affecting the plot of the story.

Script}
Setting
Scene description
Character
Dialogue
Length pace duration

Draft} once you have finished the first draft of the script you will be expected to revise the scripts outcome and wither it is ready to be filmed. You will have to consider these things first.

Outline – summarize the overall script and narrative check for any flaws And make sure that everything is in place to be filmed ensuring the perfection of the narratives continuity.

Phrases – check for any phrases in the narrative and the story ensure that they are correct and in continuity with story's dialogue, remember phrases is what connects the dialogue too the story.

Analytical opinions – discuss with peers the drafted script and take note of any floors you may have then altercate these flaws swiftly.

Level – check that the script operates at the same level so if it is a level 3 colloquial such as idiom make sure you only put the same idioms in for e.g. slander which is a negative.

Topic – is the topic being conveyed one of the six topics being assigned to you through the company's logo e.g. (slumber party) (hygiene) (challenges) (cookery) freshness (care) use one of these three topics for your script.

Meaning – is the mending related to the content asked of you is the terminology relevant to your assigned task what significance has the draft got to the final product of the script.

Issue – what issues are arising is it simple and flawless or are there moments of intricate difficulty do you have too simplify the text.

Scenario} once you have finished the first draft of your script it will be important to reflect on the topic of the scenario. This is in relation too the narrative and denotes the different types of meaning being conveyed in the script.

Scene description — what type of things is going on in the scene describe the characters briefly describe the location describe the props and describe the environment (background)

Chapters — what part of the story relates too the narratives subject matter this is all in a chapter, chapter 1 may start with a girl inviting her friends chapter 2 they come over chapter 3 they settle in the party chapter 4 they eat milk and cookies e.t.c. This is all relevant of a chapter.

Point theory — what do you do when you write next to a script you have a point theory it will be a good idea to revise this point theory and think of topical phrases and anecdotes to write next to it. This can be in the form of a word graph that will be explained in to paragraphs.

Active endeavour — in the scenes of big movies there are activities that convey the stories context and active endeavour must be reflected upon to give the story its keen nature that keeps people interested.

Certified scale} what and how are you trying to appeal to is it a younger or older audience who will be most interested in the topic you are involved in.

Target audience — who do you expect to sale to what type of audience sunrise is aimed at kids and our target audience is five to twelve.

Various associations — what would you associate with when certifying this entertainment genre something for the kids is on the agenda.

Media entertainment — what makes this genre a media entertainment module and how will this be conveyed later on.

Style — how does the style relate to a particular audience what messages are being shown to decide wither this is for the youth.

Word graph} writing can be difficult without the use of writing aids so making a word graph that relates to a theme or topic will be advised through the session.

Chart – a word diagram that insinuates a topic can be down in a session on the white board.

Features – in this case relates to quality of work simple will be the key feature on the script so remember to keep the format duty simple when drafting a script final product.

Equilibrium – how does the symmetry add up refer to a word graph to ensure the symmetry is in place correctly with the right continuity?

Analogy – is the script in comparison with the narrative has the theme been in the appropriate correspondence too the story make sure these things add up.

Metaphors – what have you done to ensure the story narrates the theme metaphors on a word graph can give you multiple episodes so look out for this type of work on your script and refer to the narrative?

Style – the style of a word graph can take many forms make sure that you have got a good style on the word graph, this will be reflected in the script.

Story objective} the objective of a story can be the most creative thing on the pages of a script, to ensure the story is entertaining you must keep an objective such as an adjective. Here are a few objectives you can take from.
Retrieval
Conquest
Investigation
Survival
Achievement

Story theme} the story theme has similarities but is a different Diegesis make sure the theme of your story here are a few too keep in mind
Vengeance
Love
Honour
Justice
Revenge
A vengeances

Production}

You are being assigned by wuning productions to film a series of scripts, you will have to write a crew and cast list budget apply for a sum of money through administration find a suitable location relating to the scripts by logistics and film performers for the purpose of distributing wuning productions digital versatile discs to media companies.

You will have to get together filming permits and permission forms for the intention of showing them to property owners specifying the dates of when and how your going to make the production, once these have been signed you will then begin filming these productions for them to be sold onto media companies.

Location research – find suitable premises for the filming of productions look at the budget of the production and cost before deciding wither the place is suitable for filming.

Form signing – sign location forms for the budget of the production and budget forms for the cost and fee of the location filming permission forms for the lease of premises.

Health and safety – health and safety forms for the hygiene and overall clarity of the production set. Risk assessment forms for the hazard and difficulty of the locations function.

Company operations – each department managers will be expected to read their contract and the company policies document and will be asked to revise whilst at wuning they will be assigned different tasks whilst at wuning everyone will be contracted to work at wuning for five years on textbooks periodicals and media presentations for the positive growth of entertainment and the community in general.

Film permission formas}
Location forms

Equipment check-lists}
Filming permits}

Cast crew

Logistics}
Travel will work in the form of travel ode and communication networking for supply and demand of location and area surveillance.

Travel costs will be put forward, through too administration and essentials sheet written up signed and dated.

A logistics manager (production officer) will be in charge of the filming and production of a feature and will have too operate the whole set.

As A LOGISTICS MANAGER AND PERSONEL YOU ARE EXPECTED TOO TRAVEL WITH TECHNOLOGICAL EQUIPTMENT SO health and safety measure will have too be applied at all times.

Location - Location managers are responsible for all the practical arrangements involved with shooting programmers, photographs and productions outside the studio.

Productions are made in a wide range of locations; location managers need to research, identify and organize appropriate sites.

As well as arranging and negotiating site use, the role usually involves managing sites throughout the shooting process.

research A location manager's role follows a sequence of activities from the pre-planning to completion stages of a production.

Typical activities include: Assessing scripts or storyboards and breaking them down into locations and a schedule.

Meeting with the director and designer to discuss projects; Collating ideas and undertaking research using resources such as the Internet, specialist location libraries, and local and regional film commissions/ agencies.

Producer} arrange set, communicate with film crew]

The second production team should have hints of creativity and the ability too post edit scripts so a shooting script will have too be arranged so the outlay of the location matches brief description.

Locations – locations will be networked and scoured across the country until the perfect place has been found too shoot film and record a script.

Director} direct scripts, adjust camera angles, use camera, and review script the second part of this brief is production and filming of script, as an assigned director you will have to ensure that any film script edits are done efficiently and that the filming continuity makes sense.

Writer} edit script on location, an on set write will have to ensure that the narrative is converted into a shooting script explaining camera angles so a close up, mid shoot, long shoot and landscape shoot a hand out will be provided.

Actors} read script, perform script, talent, performers will be instructed on what they have to do and be hired through various talent agencies.

Equipment} health and safety, risk assessment, hazard checks, equipment will have to be checked and safety verified so it would be an important process to take time assessing the risks of equipment and checking out the health and safety of various locations.

Script} continuity edits, film permits, the script is the most important asset and it would be advised that production managers assess the continuity and apply for a film permit via the council (wuning)

Location forms

Filming the production} after filling out various forms such as location forms and health and safety forms you will have to begin filming the production. You will need a number of equipment and you will have to get risk assessment forms to ensure that it is safe to use them.

Revise media equipment}

Camera crew checklist} script editor director cast talent crew

Camera operation}

Audio sound microphone} boom microphone

Set props}

Location script}

Lights} day night dark light

Tracking} camera equipments

Shooting script} (narrative) filming

Post production}
Screening

Screen theatre film analysis

Positions contract observations

Editing}

The final edit}

The final product}

Distribution}

Merchandising}

Business Plan

Office essentials —
As an office based business office products are going to need to be purchased, they will be procured and managed too maintain the regulation of the buildings contractual arrangement.

Technology- personalized computers and laptop computer accessories are also going too need too be purchased.

These things are essential for set up of an office and a business start up. Telephones and the use of the Internet are going too be important for networking and liaising with business partners and clientele.
(Another important accessory would be fax machines printers and laser scanners).

Equipment/utilities —
A desk with a comfortable chair is going too be important for an office these table and chairs will be in the style of pre-modern and sophisticated with comfortable seating.

Also a score of file-faxs with poly-pockets for the use of paperwork will be required as well as pens and stationery this is also going too be used in the office.

Cabinets and draws are going too be required for storing paper work and files into as well as briefcases and books.

Furnishing –
Staff Capacity/ set up –
Comfortable and stylish modern designs aesthetic surroundings with a spacious feng shui, office refrigerators and staff telecom in each room.

Chairs tables and lamps large arm chairs designer tables and post-modern inter textual lamps. Standard yet comfortable desk chairs are too be arranged.

Carpets/floors – The carpet must have an atmospheric décor and the floor must be arranged with ceramic plywood at some stage.

Hygienic toilets- Large ten door detached male female toilets will have too be renovated, for staff members with toiletry and sink.

Merchandising storeroom –
The merchandise storeroom will be allocated in the sho gas bar were post production is posted too take place.

Here the essentials production items will be kept for the use of staff members.
Boxes of equipment – will have to be stored in the sho gas bar such as cameras and tripods.

Building essentials - `the building is going too have too be spacious and modern, with the hope of having four buildings specializing in the same form of media.

There will be four different departments with the same focus for media pre-production production post-production and finally distribution.

Departments – four main buildings are going too be arranged into four different departments these departments are going too include a main production company were all of the powerful partners and executives start the production.

In this department we will be asserting pre –production of scripts and deciding on creativity and final draft.

The second sho-gas bar social outlet were meetings and inductions take place here staff will be at leisure and meetings will be held too decide on were the company is going too be going with its self.

The third will be v-disah were the film will be shot and logistics decide on locations and suitability, health and safety officers will be on hand too ensure that everything runs smoothly and according too plan.

The final instalment will be distribution were products are taken too be sold and advertising networks are distilled form trailers too commission meetings.

Rooms —
The departments will be split into separate rooms depending on the production teams working post. (What area of work they occupy). They will be given their task duty and professions were they must compile data and sought through regulations and procedures.

Style —
A presentable and friendly atmosphere one lit by success and happiness, Majestic responsible.

A modern cultivation will be needed too ensure a sensible atmosphere is formed red interiors for the carpet black interiors for exterior gold interiors for private places.

Capacity —
Spacious and unified, twenty employees will need too fit into the rooms comfortably and twenty-five will be working in one department.

Reservations —
A main office is reserved for high-ranking staff members fifteen private offices five shred ones.

Employees —
Employees are going too be needed too make the business work so anything from four too fifty staff can be expected too be hired.

Four major executives who are going too ensure that the four main departments are going too be run efficiently and affectively.

The next fifteen will are going too be co-executives insuring that there section of the branch is going too operate and run too a high standard adhering too what there significant bosses tell them too do.

They will also liaise with clientele and deal with recruitment staff and research assistance on inductions.

The next thirty will be on the main board and attend high class and important meetings such as staff development inductions and lectures e.t.c.

The main duties will include.
Executive,
Executive administration,
Executive management,
Executive secretary.
The next fifteen co – executives, personal assistants, administration, management, secretary, editors, sales, recruitment, logistics, technical advisor, designer, leisure, catering, recruitment officer.

The rest of the employees: will assist in the production as these representatives' staff, form the relevant departments.

Renovations – A renovations team will have too be allocated too make necessary repairs and alteration to the set up of the building.

Design – an on site (designer team) will be necessary. They will be expected too handle the renovations of the offices and buildings, the overall edit of films distribution and fashion.

Clientele – will be found by the secretary via the use of telecommunications and Internet networking. The appointed secretary of the department they have been advocated too will be expected too file reports book interviews take phone call messages and research paperwork for their boss.

Wuning contracts-

Secretary - for a secretary in the main wuning Productions Company will have too be advanced at paperwork clever with communication skills.

Work articles will have too be produced by her and a team of managers who are initially assigned too answer too her.

Instead of the mundane routine secretarial jobs of answering telephones and taking messages this secretary will answer too the highest calls of the wuning boss.

She will make connections with business people take notes and keep a file of all clientele s innate vista (profiler).

This first secretary will have the title (M.A) Managerial associate which means the managers will need her permission before they can make a vacancy or recruitment.

Log into website and submit work.

Management- the main manager is going too have a similar task as the main secretary, he is going too be ensuring that everybody is in suitable attire and is co-operating with rules and regulations and code of conduct set out by the companies main boss.